Reading Intention based Candles

By

Kabir Deepak

www.candlemgicworks.com

This book is dedicated to my Dad, who was the kindest and noblest soul. I continue to follow his path of kindness and compassion!

You can purchase Hindu intention based candles prepared by Kabir Deepak!

Please check my website
www.candlemagicworks.com

It is advisable to have an experienced person prepare your candle and bless and pray it.

Kabir Deepak specializes in preparing Hindu Intention and prayers infused candles using over 75 herbs and 50 different essential oils and Sanskrit mantras and his spiritual strength.

Your birthday, full name as it appears on birth certificate and a photo would be needed for candle preparation.

What is Candle Magic?

Candle Magic is an important and much studied science and art (which is often times wrongly associated with black magic or witchcraft).

A candle represents the focal point of your intention by invoking the power and energy of fire, a transformative element in candle magic.

None of us are unfamiliar with the candle magic. If you go down the memory lane, you can perhaps remember the intense energy you put into making your wish as you blew out your birthday candles when you were a child? That moment may have been your first practice of candle magic. You might be continuing to blow candles on each birthday and making wishes and hoping that they come true for you.

We never pause and wonder where this tradition comes from – why you wish upon candles? Why do we light candles in Church or in Synagogue or Hindu temples. Can we please deities or Gods by placing a faith and prayer candle and lighting it with the fire of our intentions and leaving it in a place of worship?

Wishing on candles and lighting candles is deeply rooted in the simplest form of magical ritual – candle magic – that has been practiced since a long time.

Birthday candles and preparing intention candles are hardly any different. In both cases, you are using wishes and intentions. The only difference is perhaps that when you are preparing candle as a firm believer in magic or a spiritual person, you are writing your intentions on petition paper and anointing candles with herbs, oils and spiritual energy instead of just 'making a wish' which sends a much more

powerful energy to Source.

Often times, people wonder what are spells and there is a misconception that spells are like Harry Potter movie spells and have to be spoken or written in some code.

Candle magic works in a way that is very intuition based, amplifying your subconscious wants/needs to aid in your spiritual manifestation.

Candle magic truly does work and it can change your life, only if you believe it can. The power of choice lays within you and you must understand that candle magic is a way to "engage" the power of your mind, spirit, soul and subconscious.

When you manifest, not only does it invoke the power of positive thinking in your mind, but it creates subconscious drive to help you achieve what you want. Yes, there are mystical forces at work in the universe that can help you get results you want; but the most power lays within you. This phenomenon is also more commonly known as the Law of Attraction, using your energy to attract what you want in your life and allow positive things to come your way.

The magic lies not just in prayers, herbs, oils, intentions but in BELIEVING in it.

Faith is the most important ingredient in Hindu candle magic. Believing in the power of magic does not mean that burning a candle with oils and herbs will instantly solve all your problems and attract all your desires.

This is not a Harry Potter's wand or spell work like Abracadabra chant and works in a fraction of a second. Also Hindu Intention based candles are not WITCHCRAFT!

Reading Signs of a Intention based Candle

What is Candle Reading?

In my last book - Candle Magic Works, I talked about preparing Hindu Intention based candles and candle magic. I decided to write a sequel to the book about signs to read and how to interpret when a candle is burning and after it has burnt.

A lot of energy interplay happens during the course of burning a candle. The wax is melting due to the heat of flame (fire element), the herbs start burning and produce a special aroma, the wick starts burning, the oils added to the candle also start reaching their point of combustion and above all, the intentions and prayers are carried through the flame of the candle and the smoke that the candle is emanating.

Besides that as the candle burns, smoke rises, there might be opposing forces and resistance to the prayers and intentions that can be visible through myriad of ways. The wick of the candle may become bifurcated or have several lobes, the candle may burn with a low flame, the glass encasing the wax may start getting darker in color due to soot deposition.

You have to analyze and understand all the factors and observe how the candle is burning. The burning candle allows you to witness your intentions in motion and hence every sight and sound needs to be carefully understood for you to able to interpret if the candle magic is working or not.

Please also listen to the sounds that the candle produces as I believe that our spirit guides, guardian angels and Gods are communicating messages. So listen carefully!

In this book, I will discuss about-

1. Reading Candle flame while it is burning

2. Understanding and reading the smoke coming out when candle is burning

3. Reading the rate at which candle is burning

4. Reading the soot color on candle

5. Understanding the sounds emanating from candle

6. Reading the wick of candle

7. Reading the wax left after candle has burnt

8. Reading the burnt herbs after candle is done burning

9. Broken candle and shattered glass

10. Reading imagery on glass

Terms used

Let's talk about a few terms that are often used for candle burning -

1. **Capnomancy** - (otherwise known as *libanomancy)* signifies a method of divination using smoke. This is done by looking at the movements of the smoke after a fire has been made. A thin, straight plume of smoke is thought to indicate a good omen whereas the opposite is thought of large plumes of smoke.

2. **Ceromancy** - It is an art of divination by wax (a word that can also refer to reading patterns formed by dripping wax into water).
It is therefore known as Capno-Ceromany or Cero-Capnomancy-- divination by smoke and wax.

3. **Pyromancy-** It is an art of divination by fire. Ancient Greeks used to predict future using fire. Hence Pyromancy is central for candle reading as the flame of the candle allows us to see the efficiency of prayers and results of prayers through the flame.

Candle reading is the practice of observing the signs and omens in the candle's behavior while it is burning and how it deconstructs in relation to the working and or the prayer spell.

Candle represents the focal point of your intentions and hence it is necessary that you pay attention to all the signs while candle is burning. Candles produce- smoke, sounds, release soot, the flame flickers, the herbs burn and produce a certain smell. It is always a good idea to read the intention based candles when they are burning and after they have burnt. Candles reveal a lot of information regarding how the prayers and intentions (often called spells by a lot of folks) have worked, what are the immediate oppositions and remittances to your prayers.

Precautions while burning candle

Here are few things to be kept in mind before you start burning candles. These precautions seem mundane but a lot of people make these mistakes and then proceed to jump to conclusions with the signs that they observe while candle is burning.

1. Ensure that the wick of the candle is trimmed and cut before you start burning the candle.

2. Do not put too much quantity of oils in the candle with the thought in your mind that too much oil will make your intentions work faster. You only need a drop or two of essential oil for the candle

3. Don't put too much herbs in the candle as they will start burning fast and in the beginning of the candle and will cause the candle glass to break.

4. Keep sufficient spacing between candles to prevent overheating and this will prevent overheated candle glass to expand and crack.

5. Make sure that candles are not place directly under a vent for AC and also not in a room with a fan that is on.

Scientific reason behind weird candle behavior

Sometimes a candle shows a weird behavior and that can be explained in scientific terms. Here is a list of abnormal and weird behavior that are observed.

1. A tall and huge flame is caused by an untrimmed wick. Make sure that you trim the wick of the candle before lighting the candle as it will prevent a very tall and large flame
2. Candle burning too fast could be due to the large wick and also too much oils in the candle.
3. Black soot is the result of excess oils and or sometimes due to the colorants used in the candle being exposed to high heat. Make sure not to add too much oils in the candle.
4. Any candle that suddenly goes out could just due to breeze. Ensure that candle should not be too close to an open window or burnt in a room with the fan switched on in the room.
5. Candles breaking too frequently is due to the fact that you are keeping a lot of candles too close to each other and since there is a lot of heat released by other candles in proximity, this is causing the candles to break. Please don't panic and keep adequate space between candles
6. We all know that physical properties of the candles cause them to burn differently from each other. So don't jump to conclusions that one spell is working faster than the other since one candle is burning faster than the other.

Reading the flame of the Hindu Intention based candles

A lot of information is revealed by the flame of the intention based Hindu prayer candles. You need to notice the flickering flame of the candles and identity the type of flame that you observe.

You can always check out my website www.candlemagicworks.com for ordering Hindu intention based candles and book a session with Kabir Deepak at www.mysticofeast.com.

We can categorize the flames of the candles as follows-

Small and weak flame

As a general rule, a small flame that flickers and bends is not a good sign in candle magic. This is a sign that the timing of the intention based Hindu candle burning could be wrong. This can also indicate that you could be praying for an outcome or a result that is unlikely or unfavorable for you in the long run. If the small flame falters or drowns in the melted wax, that is a sure sign that your petition and desire will not be fulfilled and granted at this point in time. Please don't lose hope as the universe, your spirit guides and guardian angles have a unique way of helping you and ensuring that your intentions and prayers are answered. In case, you see a very weak and small flame, you can repeat the spell after a week or on next cycle of moon, so like Full or New moon, whichever is coming next.

Dancing candle flame

Sometimes you might observe a flame that is weirdly dancing

erratically and this makes you wonder what is going on.

Whenever there is a lot of energy in the candle the candle flame appears erratic and dancing. This energy can be chaotic energy.

- Large dancing flame indicates that prayers have been answered and spells or intentions will give positive results.

- Small dancing flame means the spell may be impacted and affected by opposing forces. There might be other forces and someone else's intentions that could possibly be consciously or unconsciously working against you.

Sometimes when you watch the flame very closely you can observe the motion of flame and shapes that it is creating to be a useful tip for understanding the opposing forces and or people who are negatively impacting your intention based candles.

Candle doesn't remain lit

Sometimes a candle doesn't remain lit up despite the fact that the wick is large enough and there is no overcrowding due to herbs and oils. This is indicative of the fact that the intentions will not be fulfilled and the correct prayers and a new candle is needed.

In my experience, whenever there are a lot of opposing forces, the candles don't remain lit and in some cases it is so hard to even light up a candle. This goes on to prove that the intentions and prayers need to be changed as they won't be answered at this point in time.

There are times when I have prepared intention based candles for my clients and burnt at my altar and the candle flame would continuously go out and I would have to pray again and relight the candle. This indicates that intention is not working as there are too many negative forces.

Flickering flame

Flickering flame of a candle is enchanting to watch. Sometimes, you might observe that the candle flame is flickering. This can mean a couple of things-
1. Spirit guides and guardian angels are around and will help to achieve the intentions of the Hindu intention based prayer candles
2. Your petition and intentions will be heard and open up your energy to receive messages.
3. In traditional Wicca, it means that arguments can happen as

    emotions are high.

In *A Little book on Candle Magic*, author *DJ Conway* explains that a flickering or sputtering candle's communications can be interpreted by the four compass points-

- **North:** If the flame flickers toward the north, it's said to be an indication that the cause is a physical one, not from a spirit.

- **East:** A flame flickering toward the east indicates the mental part of your spell is working.

- **South:** The bending of the flame toward the south demonstrates a great deal of physical energy surrounds your intent.

- **West:** When the candle flame tilts to the west, it reveals the depth and energy of very strong emotions that are part of the spell work.

In my personal experience for preparing candles for my clients and burning them at my altar, I have seen that sometimes the flame is flickering intensely and I have seen very good results from that candle.

You can always buy my prepared intention based candles at www.candlemagicworks.com and book a tarot counseling session at www.mysticofest.com to understand which candle to buy.

Crackling Flame

It is not unusual to hear some weird crackling sounds emanating from a candle and in my experience over multitude of years, I have seen and heard flame of candle creating crackling sounds. In Hindu tradition, it is considered a good omen as the deities and spirit guides are communicating and you need to focus on listening to the message. A very loud crackling sound can indicate emotions are high and there are chances of arguments and small crackling sound indicates that there is a positive message from guarding angels and spirit guides.

In *A Little book on Candle Magic*, author *DJ Conway* also writes that that a flame that sputters and crackles can indicate a form of communication. The intensity of both determines the messaging. Loud crackling and frequent sputtering warns of arguments.

Noisy Sputtering Flame

I will share a story for the work I had done for someone to have success in court case. Over 11 years ago, a client scheduled a reading for understanding and discussing a legal situation that they are going through. It was a case of sexual harassment and discrimination at workplace. I finished the reading and told them that the outcome was not looking positive as there are a lot of folks around them, who were pretending to be friends but in reality were not allies.

Upon my client's insistence and against my advice, I decided to prepare a candle for success in court case in the above situation. There were few very interesting things that happened-
1. The candle would not light up and hence I changed my strategy and prepared a new candle for my client.
2. The second candle had a very tall flame and it started creating loud sputtering sounds right from the start. I advised my client to change her thought process and instead of a success candle do a **negativity removal candle**.

A noisy and continuous sputtering flame may indicate that someone or other forces oppose you. You can light additional candles to provide greater energy. If the sputtering continues, it's best to end your work and try another time.

To end the story, the negativity removal candle worked well as it came out clean and I followed it up with road opening candle, chakra balancing candle and finally success in court case candle.

In three months after doing regular candles for over 10 weeks, they received a very large sum of money as the case was won.
For candle magic to be impactful make sure to work with set of candles and repeat set of candles until energies have settled and you see a consistent positive results.

Please check my website www.candlemagicworks.com to order Hindu intention based candles.

Dual Flames

I must share another story of a client who lived in Riverside County, California, she had experienced loss of her mother a few months before she came for a tarot counseling session with me. She had hit an all time low in her life, while she was still grieving the loss of her mother, her sister was diagnosed with breast cancer as well. To make matters worse, she was laid off from work. She was very depressed and in a deeply agonized mental frame of mind.

After the tarot counseling session, she insisted to buying the right candle for herself, I explained to her that the best candle to begin with would be Anxiety Soothing candle. I prepared the candle and she took it with her to burn at her altar. Two days later, she reached out with a short video of the candle flame. I had never seen this before, the candle had two dancing flames instead of one. Such candles show that there are two energies at work, not all the time can these energies be synergistic. Sometimes two flames can represent two antagonistic and opposing energies in action.

In my client's case, the two energies were opposing as she felt that during the day her anxiety was low but as soon as it was evening, she became more anxious. I decided to work with a protection candle to remove the negative and opposing forces from around her and followed up by anxiety soothing candle. We finished set of 9 candles in 3 weeks and she not only found a new job in the third week but also her confidence was renewed.

It is a good idea to use protection candles, un-hexing, uncrossing candles to remove any negative intention and to protect your client's energy field.

Two Energies at Work

The most common interpretation for dual flames is the presence of two energies that are either working together or in opposition of each other. This is determined by the intentions that are used for the candle.

In *Coventry Magic with Candles, Oils, and Herbs*, author *Jacki Smith* discusses candles that burn with more than one flame. Aside from the natural physical causes, Smith says that the traditional interpretation of two flames burning from one wick involves two energies or energy that is cut in half.

Flame Self-Extinguishes

In my vast experience over decades, I have rarely observed that the flame extinguishes itself. In the summer of 2018, I started working with a top level executive who was afraid of being laid off due to reorganization in his company. He was certain that the axe is going to fall on his job as he was making a lot of money and the company was deciding to cut paychecks and make significant changes.

During his tarot counseling session, I saw that the coming seven weeks were tumultuous and the chances of losing job was very high. I recommended that I prepare a set a candles for - removing jealousy, banishing negativity and road opening for him.

I prepared the candles and lit them, two candles had very low flames- banishing negativity and road opening candle. I continued to chant Sanskrit mantras to add my spiritual energy. Within an hour both the candles extinguished themselves and I texted my client and asked if he was doing okay. **Self Extinguishing flame indicates that a spell or intentions are opposed by spirit realm or some other individual.**

He was very nervous and anxious as he was asked to have a meeting in following week.

Long story short, I repeated the candles and continued to work with faith and after three weeks, we found out that his job was saved but his bonus and two weeks of paid time off was removed from his contract. He heaved a sigh of relief.

According to *Candle Magic for Beginners: The Simplest Magic You Can Do* by Richard Webster, when a flame self-extinguishes, it puts an end to your work. This can also mean your prayer or spell was received by the spirit world. It can indicate that your spell is opposed by either the spirit realm or an individual.

Self extinguishing flame means that prayers would not be answered.

You can always book a session with Kabir Deepak at www.mysticofeast.com and discuss about your concerns and get recommendation for candles. Prepared candles can be bought at www.candlemagicworks.com

Steady Flame

It is a good sign of the intentions and prayers working. Good Job! Your petition and prayers will be answered.

Continue to work with Faith and not fear!

Healthy Flame

A healthy flame always has a black or red core, surrounded by a blue halo and then a yellow color.

The yellow color region which is the bright part of the flame is the middle zone. It is moderately hot and partial combustion of fuel takes place. The least hot region of the flame is present innermost. This inner zone is red or black in color due to the presence of unburnt wax vapors.

A blazing red center tells you that spirits are getting to the heart of the matter.

A red center that is dim or just a pinpoint reveals a situation that may not be motivated by the heart.

If the wick of the candle starts building a little bulb at its tip, chances are that you have opposition or a third party working against you.

If there is a lot of blue in the flame, I take that as a sign that angels and spirits are protecting you from a possibly unhappy outcome.

Please check out my website www.candlemagicworks.com to buy prepared Hindu intention based candles.

Reading the smoke
released by the candle

Reading the smoke
released by the candle

Capnomancy

A lot of smoke is released

Air is a supporter of combustion and is required for candle to burn. Almost every time you light an intention based Hindu candle, smoke is released. This smoke can be white or black in color. Sometimes a lot of smoke is released as you light the candle. Abundant smoke is neither a good nor a bad sign. It merely indicates the element of Air is present in the spell, the element of communication and observation.

When an intention based candle puts out lots of smoke, you are being called upon to use your eyes and mind to read the situation. You must look at the shape, color, timing, and movement of the smoke.

White colored smoke

When a candle releases white smoke it is considered to be a sign of blessings and benevolent spirits. If a candle breathes out a puff of white smoke, especially at a significant moment, it means that your wish will be granted. This is a good sign for the prayers to be answered and wishes fulfillment.

In many cases, I have observed that candles start burning and releasing white colored smoke and the client feels a sudden surge in positive energy and their intentions start working.

In February 2019, one of my oldest clients visited me from New York City and was in a state of dilemma, she hated her current job in NYC and wanted to move to San Diego. She had interviewed for two jobs in the last three months and there was no positive response from either of the jobs.

During the tarot counseling session, I understood the message from the Divine source that my client was under stress and needed healing and road opening. I recommend the healing and road opening candles for her. I prepared the candles for her and in three days she texted me from New York City that she got the job offer from Carlsbad company in San Diego County. In her case, it was her restless energy that was causing a lot of anxiety and I did healing candle to relax her and the road opening candle with Hindu prayers opened her roads for new job offer. Her candles released a lot of white smoke!

Black colored smoke

I have witnessed so many times when I am burning Negativity removal candles for some of my clients that a dense black smoke is released.

Dense, black smoke coming from an intention based candle means negative energy.

Conflict, bad luck, and opposing purposes surround your intentions and prayers. It is a good idea to spend some time in prayer or meditation and do a cleansing ritual before proceeding with the working.

In such cases, I recommend aura cleansing using my special herbs and oils for the client. A good cleansing and protective candle, followed by negativity removal candle often seem to do the trick in majority cases.

Please book your tarot counseling session and a cleansing session with Kabir Deepak at www.mysticofeast.com.

You can also purchase prepared Hindu intention based candles at www.candlemagicworks.com

Direction of Candle smoke

As soon as I light the intention based prayer candles, I often observe the direction of candle smoke. It is very essential to observe the direction of smoke being produced by candle as it reveals a lot about the fact that if the intentions and prayers would be answered.

1. If the candle smoke wafts towards you it means that your prayer is more than likely to be answered. This is always a good sign.

2. If the candle smoke wafts away from you, then it means that you will need a great deal of patience for your prayers to be answered.

3. If the candle smoke blows to your left it means that you are getting too emotionally involved with the situation and are in danger of subconsciously sabotaging your own prayer so that it may not be answered.

4. If the candle smoke blows to the right then it means that you will need to use your head rather than your emotions to pursue the situation.

Rate at which candle burns

Believe it or not, candles burn at different rates even though they might start at the same time. This is a common occurrence and I have seen it many times happen in front of my eyes. Look at the picture below in which there are three candles started at same time on left

and remaining five candles on right started at same time.

The candles are not only burning at different rates but also, show different soot deposited. We will discuss about soot deposition in the next chapter.

Why do candles burn at different rates?

Candles whose spells or intentions are working faster start burning at a faster rate. There are so many forces and factors involved in the the rate of burning.

Sometimes candles that burn create craters in the middle of the candle. This is most common with large pillars and container candles, but it can also happen with votives and other candle shapes.

The melted wax is centered closely around the wick, leaving tall walls of wax on the sides.

Nobody likes it when a candle burns incompletely, and it's not a good sign in candle magic, either.

It usually means that your intentions are very weak to cast an effective spell or prayers at this time. Or that the spell's energies have been blocked from reaching their intended target.

Color of soot deposited on candle

All candles are made up of wax except for soy candles. Wax is made up of hydrocarbons or simply made from the elements Carbon and Hydrogen. When wax burns it produces- Carbon dioxide, water vapor, unburnt wax particles, smoke and unburnt carbon particles called soot.

Now it is noteworthy and very interesting that some candles have black smoke and soot deposited and some candles burn clean and clear. While others have some cloudy soot or white soot on them.

Black smoke on the glass, a dirty sooty burn

As a general rule, black smoke or black soot on the candle is not considered a good sign as it reveals blockages and obstacles in general. I call them resistance and opposition to spells. You should always look for following signs-

1. Black soot is on the top and if the black soot does not travel all the way down the glass, and is only at the top or perhaps stops in the middle, the negative influence or obstacle has been unblocked. The intentions or spells had opposition in the beginning but they have been overcome after initial resistance to spell.

2. Black soot on entire length, it means your intentions, spells and prayers have been blocked and there are still forces preventing you for attaining your desired result. It could also indicate someone has casted a spell against you. In such cases, I recommend to burn another candle to break through their defenses.

3. Black soot is at the bottom of the candle, it is a warning that negative influences are being sent to you. There are many challenges facing you and there is a tough road ahead. Someone(s) may be working against you. At the top of the glass on the inside, take a sharp object and inscribe the symbol of your spiritual comfort – such as a cross or OM sign – all the way around or in front and back. I recommend accelerating your protections and start a series of uncrossing rituals.

Whenever, I come across black soot on candles, I recommend the clients to allow me to prepare another set of candles to combat with negativity and resistance and opposition sent to them. It is a good idea to repeat the intention based candles until the candles burn clean.

White smoke on the glass

Sometimes, candles have white soot deposited on them.

White soot indicates spiritual communication, purity, and positivity. It could also indicate that the spirits and Gods have heard your prayers and removed the negativity from the working. This is especially true in un hexing or uncrossing rituals. It is always a good idea to observe the white soot on candles.

1. If the <u>white soot only goes half way down or less,</u> the cleansing was successful. The candle has worked well and the results are positive.

2. If the <u>white soot is carried through the length of the candle</u> you may need further cleansing and spiritual work. I often recommend repeating the intention based candle.

3. If the <u>soot is at the bottom of the candle</u>, it signifies the presence of outside aid or help either spiritually or physically. This is a good sign but spell or intention based candle should still be repeated.

4. If the <u>candle burned half black and half white</u>, this means that one aspect is overriding the other. Look to which is on top to see what was undone. If black is on top, your spirit guides cleared it. If white is on top the spirit guides of another person who has hexed or cursed you or is causing problems to you, have combated your attempts. It is a good idea to repeat the intention based candles, until it burns clear or has uniform white soot on glass of the candle.

5. If the <u>white soot is on only one side of the candle</u>, this is a sign that what you are doing is incorrect. Either the candle preparation wasn't appropriate or the spirits aren't happy with the candle itself.

Please check www.candlemagicworks.com to buy prepared candles, candles will be customized and blessed with Kabir's Sanskrit mantra prayers, anointed with special essential oils and herbs with the right vibration to make your intentions come true.

Please ensure that spell or intentions are not violating or manipulating FREE WILL. I refuse to do LOVE SPELLS and spells or intentions for inflicting pain or harm to anyone as Karma will come back to haunt ten times more to you.

Sounds coming from candle

Candles produce sounds while burning. These can range from-

1. Popping sounds to

2. Crackling sounds

When you hear popping sounds that are not too loud it indicates that the guardian angels and spirit guides are working on your intentions and answering your prayers. The popping sounds can also be created by burning of herbs and you should place your ears close to candle to listen to the sound of candle.

Loud crackling sounds are indication of arguments and chaos around you as emotions of people around you would be high. This can be frustrating and disturbing, in such a situation, make sure to pray on the candle.

Reading the wick of the candle

The wick of the candle, while the candle is burning reveals a lot about the spell and intentions in action.

Notice carefully and you will find that sometimes the wick is globular or has a bulb or is divided into small bulbs in different directions.

This is not a good sign as it indicates that there is someone else who is working against you in the form of ill-intentions, cursing, evil eye, casting a black magic spell, creating opposition in work etc.

Please don't take this lightly as spell will have to be repeated.

Please buy your prepared candles from www.candlemagicworks.com and you can also book a tarot counseling session with Kabir Deepak on www.mysticofeast.com

Wax residue left

When working with intention based candles, it is necessary to notice if any wax residue is left on the candle. This is not a great sign as it shows opposition coming from within you. You should pray and work with faith.

When a candle leaves wax residue

If there is around 1/2" or more in the bottom, the spell needs to be repeated.

Wax on the sides of the glass indicates where there are personal hindrances to the progress of the spell.

Accelerated Burn

This is considered a good sign, however the rewards may be short lived and the spell will need to be repeated.

Herbs burnt

Herbs are a big component in the candle and they amplify the intentions and prayers of the clients. Choosing the right herbs for candles is a difficult task and should be performed by an experienced person. I choose from over 75 Indian herbs to dress the Hindu Intention based prayer candles.

Herbs should be used in dry form only. Sometimes, if you over use herbs and they catch fire in the beginning of the candle burning, then it can cause the candle to break from the top.

Make sure to speed the herbs evenly around the wick and not allow overcrowding. Ideally, the herbs should burn in the end only.

When herbs burn, they produce a characteristic aroma and it fills the air with a pleasant smell and the smoke of burning herbs carries your intentions to the universe.

Herbs should burn completely and if they are not burnt completely it indicates that the spell has not worked well as the energies of herbs were not harassed properly and the spell and candle needs to be repeated.

Glass shattered or

broken

It is not a common phenomenon for the glass of the candle to break or explode. I hardly see that happening, maybe once in a few months I have witnessed broken candle and a candle completely exploded. It is quite rare and can be disturbing.

1. If the candle glass cracks but does not break it means there was some opposition that was broken. It may have been sent to the spell to try to deflect it or it may have been encountered along the way. It is not a bad sign for the crack in the beginning or in the middle but it is bad if the crack happens in the end of the candle burning.

2. If the candle glass does not break or shatter then the spell is protected and was successfully defended.

3. However, if the candle glass breaks or shatters it means you are up against something negative and the spell and intentions have a lot of opposition. It also means that malicious forces have been attracted to your intentions and are trying to interfere. It can also indicate someone is casting negative intentions and spells against you and you are not spiritually protected or strong enough as what was thrown at you was larger than what you were sending out.

Either way, I recommend to do a stronger spell or intention based candle to combat the negativity sent your way.

Blockages could be the result of someone coming up against you, however you could be creating the blockage yourself thus sabotaging your spell.
Make sure to book an appointment with Kabir Deepak at www.mysticofeast.com to discuss further.

Imagery on candle glass

You will be shocked to see the complex imagery that appears on a burnt candle sometimes. It can range from a face of a person to a letter or alphabet in English or a different language as well. Sometimes it shows more than one person and energy that is trying to prevent your intentions and prayers to be fulfilled and answered.

In my vast experience, I have handled many situations where I have seen the starting alphabet of a name and or the gender of the person and the facial features to finer details and let my clients know who they are up against.

Please pay special attention to faces, images and alphabets that appear on a burnt candle.

Book an appointment with Kabir Deepak at www.mysticofeast.com for reading a candle.

Before starting any candle work it is a good idea to book a session with **Kabir Deepak** at www.mysticofeast.com to assess the current situation and find out what candles would be needed or if any candle magic work is needed for your current situation.

Don't do candle magic with half baked information available these days on youtube by self proclaimed witches and candle magic practitioner as they may not have experience about what they are doing and it might impact your energy field in a negative way. Please refrain from doing any spells to bring back your ex and or Love spells using candle magic unless you are in a committed relationship and your partner loves you and you want to solidify your relationship.

Candle magic should NEVER be used for manipulating free will!

It is always a good idea to use prayers, herbs, essential oils and blessings of an experienced person to prepare candle for you.

Check out www.candlemagicworks.com for buying prepared candles by Kabir Deepak.

Many Blessings and prayers!

Made in the USA
Las Vegas, NV
12 September 2024

95195152R00026